The ABCs of BEING a TEENAGER

LOIS COOK PETERSON

BROADMAN PRESS
Nashville, Tennessee

© Copyright 1988 • Broadman Press
All rights reserved
4247-05
ISBN: 0-8054-4705-9
Dewey Decimal Classification: 155.5
Subject Heading: ADOLESCENCE
Library of Congress Catalog Card Number: 87-36464

Printed in the United States of America

LIBRARY OF CONGRESS
Library of Congress Cataloging-in-Publication Data

Peterson, Lois Cook, 1952-
   The ABCs of being a teenager / Lois Cook Peterson.
     p. cm.
   Summary: An alphabetically arranged survey of issues and concerns
facing teenagers, including alcohol, grades, jobs, parents, self-
esteem, and zits.
   ISBN 0-8054-4705-9 (pbk.)
   1. Adolescence—Juvenile literature. 2. Teenagers—Life skills
guides—Juvenile literature. [1. Adolescence—Dictionaries.]
I. Title.
HQ796.P4636   1988
305.2'35—dc19   87-36464
                                                                               CIP
                                                                               AC

With love and gratitude
to my parents

Preface

Being a teenager is both exciting and tough. It is exciting because you feel you are finally reaching the age where some of your goals seem possible. It seems tough because, though you feel like you're growing up, others don't always treat you that way. The decisions you have to make are also getting harder and harder.

This book is meant as a guide and support for your teenage years. I hope you will learn your questions have answers, the difficulties you have are common to others, and the future is in your hands. You can start making some of your dreams come true right now.

Contents

A Adolescence, Alcohol, Always, Answers 11
B Body (Yours), Books, Brothers 15
C Change, Choices, College, Courage 18
D Dating, Disappointment, Dreams, Drugs 22
E Exercise, Expectations, Exploring 26
F Feelings, Friends, Future 29
G God, Grades, Graduation 32
H Heroes, Home, Homework 36
I Impatience, Infatuation, Interest 39
J Jealousy, Jobs, Justice 42
K Kindness (to others), Kindness (to self) 45
L Laughter, Losing, Luck 48
M Mistakes, Money, Moving, Mystery 51
N Never, No, Nutrition 55
O Opportunities, Organization, Overcoming, Overload 58
P Parents, Peer Pressure, Perfection, Personal
   Problems, Plans 62

Q Questions, Quiet Times 67
R Rainbow, Relaxation, Religion 69
S Self-esteem, Shyness, Sisters, Suicide 72
T Talents, Teachers, Tests 76
U Unbelief, Understanding 79
V Vocation, Volunteer 81
W Why? Winning, Worry 83
X eXcitement, eXtremes 86
Y Yes, You 88
Z Zeal, Zits 90
Summary 92

A

Adolescence

Adolescence is a word you may have heard only recently. What is adolescence, anyway? It stands for the period of time when a person grows from childhood to adulthood. It covers a very important period of your life because during adolescence you begin to make important decisions on your own. You begin to learn who you really are. You make decisions that could affect the rest of your life. Adolescence is looked on by some with fear, some with gladness, others with excitement. Whatever way you feel, what happens during your teen years is very important to you.

Being a teen can be difficult, but it can be equally exciting. You are entering upon a period of your life when you will change physically, socially, mentally, and spiritually. Sometimes these changes will surprise you; sometimes they may frighten you; and always, they can be signs of greater things yet to come. Don't be afraid to seek help and information when you need it. You aren't the first person to live through adolescence, and you won't be the last. Also, you won't face anything someone else hasn't already faced! You aren't ever really alone!

Take this time as an opportunity to learn about yourself and the world, get an education, and have fun! Use this book to help make your dreams come true!

Alcohol

Few topics are more controversial than the subjects of drugs. Alcohol is one of the more controversial topics because it is legal for people to buy. Legality doesn't change the fact that alcohol is a drug. As with other drugs, alcohol can be dangerous.

Some decisions a person makes have long-term consequences he can't see at the time decisions are made. Deciding to drink is one such decision. You may do it because your peer group is pressing you. That's a short-term decision. Your peer group is here and now. The long-term results can be alcoholism. Read the biography of a alcoholic and you read about a person with a unpleasant life. An alcoholic sometimes loses his friends, his job, and his family. That's sounds like a heavy price for a "high," doesn't it? There are other ways a person can get "high" on life.

Trouble can still follow you if you don't become a alcoholic. Imagine if one night you have one drink too many. On the way home you have a wreck. You live, but your best friend riding in the car with you doesn't. Can you live with that? Before any decision is made, it is wise to look at all the possible consequences, not just those that seem to occur most often. Maybe you'll never have a wreck. What if you do?

At one time or another during your teen years, you will be offered alcohol. When this happens your response should depend on what you think best. It's your body. It's your life. What makes a drug dangerous is how and why the person uses it, not its legal status. Alcohol is one of those choices best left until you're "old enough" to buy it legally, at least. Even then, ask yourself if alcohol can give you something you really want. (See Drugs.)

Always

Always is a big word. It allows for no exceptions. Few things are for always. This does not always seem the case. If you have worked for something a long time and failed to get it, it may seem that you will always have to do without. Let's say you have always wanted to beat a particular student at school in something. Whatever the reason, you want to beat him at something. So, you decide the next composition contest in English will be the time. You work hard. The day comes for the teacher to announce the winner, and you "lose" again. Consider two ideas. Do you really need to beat the person, or do you need to succeed at something? Perhaps you're jealous of a skill he has which you don't. Perhaps you'd just like to see him "knocked down to size."

Here are some more examples of times teens say "always" that won't hold true. "I'll always lose out." "I'll always be dumber than Joe or Jane." "I'll always be poor." "I'll always be ugly."

"I'll always," is often expressed by someone who is not satisfied with how his or her life is going. There is nothing wrong with being dissatisfied. What is important is what you do if you are unhappy. Instead of comparing yourself with others and setting yourself up for an "I'll always," make a plan to accomplish something you wish you could do. Let's say you feel English is your worst subject. Instead of saying, "I'll always be poor in English," ask your school counselor if you could get a tutor to help you. Maybe a friend who is good in English can help you.

Always doesn't have to be. Most things can be changed. It may take time, but that's to be expected. The deciding factor is you, and you can get help if needed. You don't have to do it alone. That is always the truth.

Answers

All teens look for answers. You are becoming more aware of the world around you, and you don't always like what you find. Some questions you have can be answered now. You may find the answer in a book. Your parents may have the answer. A friend may be able to tell you why. You may have to talk to a teacher, counselor, your minister, or some other person considered to be an expert. Wherever you look for an answer, try to think of the best person to ask. Realize there are many people you can ask, not just family or friends.

You are not wrong to seek answers. You are wise to seek answers from those who will be objective about your decision. Being objective means they give you the facts and let you make up your own mind.

Try to think of the reason you need the answer. This might tell you something you need to know. For instance, let's say your best friend just left you for another person. You think it's your fault. However, your old friend and you may be developing different interests. Your old friend may have a problem. The change in your friendship doesn't have to be your or anybody's fault; it may be a natural result of changes that occur in life.

Check out any answer before going along with it. Any answer found must be checked against the things you know are true. Does it make sense? Does it go against any values you hold dear?

Some questions require that you go ahead and live the best you can, learning from other's mistakes or accidents but not becoming obsessed with them. Only Johnny knows why he killed himself. The hard part is knowing the difference between what you can know and what you can't. One of the toughest questions people seek to answer is, "Why?" (See Why?)

B

Body (Yours)

You only get one. Your body is not like a car or a stereo. When it wears out or is damaged, you can't trade it in or buy a new one. The one that you have is the one your're stuck with.

Too short. Too tall. Too skinny. Too fat. Some things about your body you cannot change. Some things you can change. Just look around at your classmates and friends. How many of them wish something were different about their bodies? You'll never know because they keep their secret desires to themselves, like you don't mention to them the things you wish were different. You can assume, however, that every person alive has, at one time or another, wished something were different about his physical characteristics.

Instead of wishing for differences, consider your good points. Do you have your health? Some don't. Can you see, walk, hear? Have you adjusted to the handicaps you do have? If not, why? What can you do to accept what can't be changed?

For those characteristics you aren't happy with, what can you change? How? Make a plan and follow it, improving the plan when necessary. You must live with you. Make your plan for change according to your needs and wishes, not the wishes of others. If everyone else is happy but you're not, what have you gained? Regardless of how you look on the outside, the important thing is how you look on the inside. Some physical characteristics can be changed, for example, being out of shape or being overweight. Other characteristics can't and shouldn't be changed, for example, being tall instead of short or having hazel eyes instead of blue. Do what changing you chose to do for yourself, not others. Keep in perspective what is really important —your inside.

Books

Books can be a blessing to your life. You probably already have favorite books: books with characters you love and pull for, books on topics that you are very interested in. Books should be an important part of everyone's life. They can give you information, inspiration, and relaxation.

One caution to consider: Be as careful about the books you read as you are about the food you eat. Books can be considered part of the diet of the mind. Whenever you read a book, ask yourself what the overall meaning is. Determine for yourself whether you think the book is realistic or true. Without realizing it, you may already be doing this. Not all books speak the truth. Regardless of what book you read, you can learn from it. However, what you might learn is how not to act or how not to be. Just like when you watch someone else, you can decide you will not behave as they do.

Books, for the most part, can add in a positive way to your life. Save your favorites. Go back and read them again. Ask friends about books they recommend. Reading is an important skill in today's world. It allows you to keep up with what is going on and allows you to make important decisions wisely.

Read. It's good for you.

Brothers

One of the common conflicts within families is between brothers and sisters. It's quite possible the expression "Oh, brother!" came from a sister trying to deal with the antics of her brother. You may find this hard to believe right now, but one day you and your brother may be friends. In fact, in some families parents say, "Fight among yourself at home if you must; but outside of this house, take up for each other." Even though it may seem impossible, try not to do anything unfair to your brother right now. One of the greatest things in the world is to have brothers and sisters who stand by each other. Not everyone has this during their teen years, or afterward.

As for brothers and brothers, you may even be friends as you grow. This is as common as brothers not getting along until they leave home and start their own careers and families. If he is older, you may admire him; if he is younger, you may feel he gets in the way. He is still your brother.

Why is it so hard to get along with your brother? Competition for your parents' affection may be one reason. You may feel your brother gets more attention than you do, whether he does or not. You may also be jealous of your brother, whether there is need to be or not. If you really feel you are being treated unfairly, tell your parents. They may see things differently or know something you don't. They may not realize they are being unfair. Parents aren't perfect, even though you may want them to be.

Find some way to communicate with your brother too. Someday you may want to and not know how anymore. (See Sisters.)

C

Change

One thing can be said about life. It changes. Little will remain the same. Just imagine how much life has changed since your grandparents were born. Sit down with them and listen to how things were when they were born—no compact disc players, no electricity in some areas, no television. What were schools like?

What do you think will happen in the next ten, twenty, or thirty years? How will schools change? What jobs will cease to exist? What will cars look like?

Regardless of what will change, some things will remain the same. People will have the same needs and wants. From the early days of man, these things have not changed. This will stay true for the future as well.

Take a moment to notice how you've changed since you started school. One day you will look back to when you were a teen and think about how fast times have changed.

In the years to come, whether you change for the positive or negative is up to you. One of the most important skills you can learn is how to adapt to change. You will have the same needs, but your ability to fulfill those needs improves. Don't get too impatient. Have fun along the way. But remember to look to the future too! Today's decisions can affect tomorrow. (See Impatience.)

Choices

One thing is sure, you have some control over your life. The choices you make do determine the kind of life you have. No matter what circumstances you live under, you can make your life something special. The choices you make are the difference between a life well spent and one wasted. Two people born in the same kind of home with the same physical characteristics, the same mental abilities, and living in the same community can end up with two completely different lives. One will be a resounding success, the other a resounding failure. The reason? The choices they made. Being rich is not a guarantee of success. Being pretty is not everything. Being smart won't mean much if you don't make good choices.

How do you make good choices? Many times you know which choice is best. Following through with your decision may not be easy, but you know what's best. When you don't know, ask yourself some basic questions. What do I want or need? How will the decision affect my life? How has it affected other people's lives? Have I asked for the opinion of people I trust and respect—parents, teachers, family, friend, peers, my minister? Many sources of information and guidance are available. What are your values? Where do they guide you? Keep in mind that everyone makes decisions that don't work out from time to time. The difference in something working out and something not working out is often the willingness of the person to persevere, to never quit.

Do you realize the choices you have? Every day you make choices. As you grow older, you will make more and more. Some, of course, are more important than others. Take more time for these, looking at long-time as well as short-term possibilities. Choices lead to possibilities.

College

Are you thinking about going to college? It just might be a good idea. College is not for everyone, but for many students college will be required for the kinds of jobs that will be available when they graduate. Some researchers estimate that by the last of this century three out of every four jobs will require some kind of education after high school.

Many students and parents worry about whether they can afford college. Costs go up every year. Some students save money for college. They open a savings account at the bank where they put part of what they earn at baby-sitting or mowing lawns or doing other part-time jobs. This money is helpful, especially for students whose parents cannot afford to pay all college expenses.

Some students do not have to pay for their college education. They earn scholarships. Academic scholarship are awarded to students whose grades and school leadership show excellence. Athletic scholarships are offered to student-athletes who prove they can make the grades and do well at a particular sport. Many kinds of financial help are available. Whether you earn a scholarship or not, just about any student can attend a college of some type. Many students work their way through college!

If you think you might want to go to college, don't give up if it looks like it will be hard to do. Keep your grades up at school, join some clubs or youth organizations, and start looking for possible scholarships your freshman year in high school. Until then save some of the money you earn. Realize that, even if your parents don't have the money, you can work summers between school years. There is no reason you can't attend college, and many reasons to work so you can attend. (See Graduation, Talents.)

Courage

Courage. What does it mean to be courageous? For many the word stands for heroes in war who are fighting for their country's freedom, risking their lives. Others think of courage as a characteristic firemen show when they go into a burning building to save a child or when a policeman risks his life to stop a crime. These individuals may be courageous. But you don't have to risk your life to show courage.

You are also courageous when you take a chance and make friends with a new student at school. You're courageous when you join the debate team but feel weak in the knees when you speak in front of a group. Courage is shown when a person takes a risk. This risk can be personal or physical.

When you take personal risks, you may risk becoming unpopular or failing to make a sport team you want to make. Physical risks involve taking a chance of being injured or worse.

There is another point to consider about courage. Being courageous doesn't mean you aren't scared. You can do something courageous and be scared at the same time. Being courageous doesn't mean you're unafraid. Being courageous means you take the chance even though you are scared. (See Peer Pressure.)

D

Dating

You may have had your first date or you may be waiting for your first. Everyone is nervous the first time. You can be nervous the first time you do anything. Dating allows you to practice social skills. It is a chance to learn more about people in general and yourself in particular. It can and should be fun. Dating is also a place many teens find peer pressure, pressure to do things that can be dangerous or stupid.

Some teens can't wait until they can have a real date, not just an occasion where their friends meet at the skating rink and pair off. Some teens are in too much of a hurry to date. They think dating proves they're grown up. They may even use dating as a way to "get back" at their parents. Dating is just like anything else. You can do it for good or not so good reasons.

Do you disagree with some of the guidelines your parents set for you? Dating is one area where your parent's rules can prove very helpful. If you don't like someone you're with, you can use your parent's rules to help "get out of the situation."

Dating is also a time when you can show your parents just how mature you are. Show by your actions that you are mature enough to do what your parents want you do.

As with any new experience, take things slow. Double date with a friend. Meet the "crowd" at the movies or the game. Know a little about the person before you offer or accept a date. Dating is a part of many exciting experiences you can have as you explore your world. It's not meant to be more important than anything else.

Disappointment

Disappointed? Has something not worked out you thought for sure would? Have you found out something about someone you just can't believe? It's hard to be disappointed. One way to define disappointment is "the feeling that someone or something has failed you, let you down."

One of the most important things to remember is that no one is perfect. Even parents are human. When you were younger, you may have thought your parents were invincible. It wasn't easy when you found out there where things they couldn't do. Sometimes the hardest disappointments of all have to do with family or friends. If you could depend on anyone it should be them! Right?

Some events and circumstances can't be changed. This in itself can be disappointing. Learning to know the difference between something you can change and something you can't change is one of the hardest lessons. When you do, you won't be as disappointed as often.

As with any problem, you can live with disappointment. What can be done? What can't? Are you asking for the impossible? Are you being fair? If you can't find the answer on your own, seek help. Ask a friend, someone you trust. You might find out there is a tomorrow after all. (See Personal Problems.)

Dreams

Everyone should have a dream. This is one way in which a person is different from animals—having a sense of fulfillment. One's life is more than sleeping, eating, and adding to the species' population. The happiest healthiest humans are those who have learned that dreams are important and have found ways to make their dreams come true.

Dreams give you something to look forward to. Make your dream come true by doing something besides dreaming; take some action. What can you do right now to start making your dream come true? You don't have to wait till you are older. Start now! Take a look at what you'd like to do. What can you do at home, school, church, or in your community to help your dream come true? You can take steps right now to make the world a better place.

Don't have a dream? Feel useless? Don't know which direction to turn? Don't sell yourself short. Everyone, yes, everyone has talents and gifts to share with others. One way to think of a dream for yourself is to consider what you would do if you could do something right now without having to wonder about failure or the costs involved?

Use your teen years to explore the activities, skills, or causes you're interested in. Let it be a time for preparation and practice. What are your dreams? Look for ways now to make them come true. (See Talents.)

Drugs

Each generation has had to deal with the issue of drugs. Your generation is not the first and won't be the last. Whether you're the first time in your life, you are making major decisions that can affect the rest of your life. You are having to make more and more decisions on your own. You are becoming more and more involved in running your own life.

You can explore your world in many ways. Some ways are smart, like choosing a hobby or joining a club. Other ways are dumb and dangerous, like driving too fast or trying cocaine. Part of life is learning to make decisions, and some of the decisions you make will involve how you can best explore yourself and your world safely.

Exploring can be spooky or scary from a personal standpoint. What if you find out you hate the job you always thought you wanted? What if you make yourself look foolish? Don't automatically give up a dream because you don't like some small tasks it involves. No matter what job you choose, there will be tasks you'd rather not do. As for looking foolish—there isn't a person alive that hasn't done that at one time or another.

Learn from experience. Keep in mind that you will be better off than your peers who refuse to take even one chance. It might be said that the fool is the person who never tries, who never takes a chance.

Expectations

Your expectations are the way you see the events, happenings, occurrences that are possible in your future. Your expectations can be for the near future, such as next week or month; they can be for the distant future, years from now.

Expectations can be good or bad. Which they are depends on how you look at life and how you think things might change. Change can be for good or bad. The idea is to act and plan in such a way that the changes you make are good ones.

The kinds of expectations you hold also depend on how you look at yourself. Are you dissatisfied? Are you fairly happy with your life? Are you very happy? A person who feels bad about himself or the world will have a hard time having good expectations.

Teens often forget two things: You can change many of the things that exist now, and others have felt the same way you do.

Learn to have great expectations. You won't get everything you want, but you can make a difference. You can take steps today to make a better tomorrow for yourself and others! Being able to dream is important to your well-being. What do you want to see happen? What do you expect to see happen? (See Dreams, Luck, Plans.)

Exploring

What is exploring? Exploring involves ways of searching, learning about, and discovering skills and abilities you have. It means becoming better aware of your abilities and inabilities and becoming better aware of the world in general. As a teenager you could say almost everything you do is a form of exploring. For

E

Exercise

When most people think of exercise, they think of exercising the body. This is definitely something everyone should do. You only get one body; you can't turn it in for a new model if you wear this one out. Abuse your body and it'll return the favor.

Another kind of exercise is also needed. It's as important to keep your mind in shape as it is to keep your body in shape. The two work together and depend on each other. An unhealthy body can adversely affect a healthy mind, and vice versa. Many different ways exist to exercise your body: walk, hike, bike, run, do aerobics. Take your choice. Different exercises exist for different personality and body needs.

To exercise your mind put healthy, positive, upbeat ideas in it. Use it. Expand in your understanding and knowledge. Read good books. Talk with people who are trying to learn each day, people with positive outlooks on life. A mind not used can become like a body not used, weak or worse—diseased.

People who keep body and mind strong can enjoy life more and be better prepared for crisis. How do you exercise your body? Sitting in front of the TV doesn't count. How do you exercise your mind? Is your mind mush? Don't just sit there! Do something!

talking about legal drugs or illegal drugs, sooner or later you will have to decide for yourself how you feel. Drugs, for good or bad, alter how your body is presently working.

Usually when someone brings up the issue of drugs to you they are referring to the use of illegal drugs, such as heroin, marijuana, or uppers and downers (amphetamines or barbiturates). In addition, they may be talking about drugs which can be bought legally (if you are old enough), such as alcohol and cigarettes, which can still be and frequently are abused. Also, don't assume that because you can buy something over the counter at the drugstore that you shouldn't be careful of its use. Many people have become addicted to medicines their doctor prescribe or over-the-counter drugs that they became too dependent on.

Ask the following questions if you think a drug has taken over your life or the life of a friend. Have the drugs affected the way I deal with other people? Am I getting along with my parents and family differently than before? How has the drug affected the way I live from day to day? Does the drug affect how well I am doing at school or at play or at work? If the drug is taking over your life, making you do things differently than you did before, look again. Drugs were never meant to be the most important thing is a person's life!

People use drugs for many reasons. Before using any drug, ask yourself why you plan to use it. If the reason is peer pressure or the inability to deal with a crisis, look again! There are better reasons for doing something!

F

Feelings

Feelings come in two varieties: those you like to have and those you wish would go away. Feelings are a part of what makes you human. You have feelings animals don't and can't have. Also, as a human, you are capable of choosing how you respond to your feelings. Animals react by instinct, not by decision making and choice. A person can examine her feelings, determine the cause, and decide if a change is necessary.

Understanding what feelings are and how they affect you helps you know what should be done. It is said you should "be in touch with your feelings." What does this mean? Sometimes an event or situation affects you and you don't realize it, at first. For example, have you ever felt bad and didn't know why? If you knew what was bothering you, you could take action to solve your problem. A person who neglects how he feels and lets his emotion build up inside can "explode." The "explosion" often shows up in some activity that is dangerous to the person himself and often others, as well. This is what can happen to someone who hasn't developed a healthy attitude toward his feelings.

How you feel affects your mental and physical health. Your feelings can tell you of problems you should handle. Use them to your advantage. It's OK to be sad, upset, or angry. How you feel is important, but why you feel a certain way and what you are going to do about it is more important. See your feelings as a way to discover what you need. Good and bad feelings are part of being human. Learn to use them to your advantage.

Friends

Everyone needs a friend. Having just one person to talk to who can help you through the rough times is important. Mental health experts say that a person with a strong support system (a group of trusted friends one can count on) can cope with life's changes and crises better than someone without a support system.

The fact is, almost everyone would like to have more friends. Real friends aren't that easy to come by. Some people pretend to be friends when they're not. What is a good test to see if someone is a real friend? Do they let you be you? Do they pressure you to do stupid or dangerous things? Do they allow you an opinion even if it's different than theirs? Can they keep a secret you've ask them to keep?

Teens often feel everyone has more friends then they do. Alone on a Friday or Saturday night, they imagine everyone else in town is out having a good time. Believe it or not, other teens are in their homes thinking the same thing. Keep in mind, however, that being alone doesn't have to mean being lonely and being in a crowd doesn't mean you won't feel lonely.

Why is the issue of friends so important? Why do parents become concerned about the friends their children have? Besides the fact that it is good for one to have friends, the kinds of friends one has can make a difference in how one's life turns out. Do your friends help you feel good about yourself? Do they make you feel good about life? If not, why? The wrong friends can lead you to bad decisions; even worse. The right friends can lead you to challenges and successes and good feelings about yourself and the world. Which do you have?

Future

When teens think about the future, two ideas come to mind: What will I do when I grow up? and Will the world even be here when I grow up?

For many teens looking toward the future means thinking about what they want to do as adults. What career do you think you would enjoy? What skills or talents do you feel you have? How will you fit into the scheme of things? In our country more than any other, an individual can make a difference. You can do things now that will help you discover your skills and how to use them. Take time during your teen years to explore and find out more about yourself and the world. Many exciting and wonderful things are happening.

The future is also frightening to many teens. They see wars and conflicts and wonder if the world will even be around for them to grow up in. To you the world may seem out of control. This has been a fear of many generations, and the world is still around today. Just imagine what some of the other generations had to endure. People by the hundreds died of smallpox. The bubonic plague in Europe killed one fourth of the population! Another idea to keep in mind is that television and newspapers tend to cover the spectacular. Many great events happen each day that are never reported.

You can make a difference in the world now and in the future. You can start by doing something positive in your own community. Join a group that is trying to work to make the world a better place. If the future frightens you to the point you can't seem to go on, find someone to talk to. Share your feelings with someone you trust who seems to be able to deal with life as it is. The world is not hopeless. (See Talents, Vocation, Volunteering, Why?)

G

God

At some time in life, each person must make a decision about God. Some people have had such desperate lives that they search for God with all their energy. Others think of God only when trouble strikes. Still others communicate with God every day and consider Him a close friend. You may see God as a grandfatherly figure or as an invisible Spirit with no form. Your mental image of God doesn't matter as much as what you believe about God.

When you want to know someone better, you can do three things. Read something the person wrote, talk to people who know that person, and talk to the person. To know God better, you can do the same three things.

Many start by reading the Bible. This may be because they don't know anyone who knows God. Reading the Bible is one of the best ways to know more about God. Pick a translation that is easy to understand and that has a concordance to help you find verses on subjects of interest to you.

Another way to know God better is to talk to people who know God. They can tell you from personal experience and their beliefs what they think God is like. Speak with someone who believes in God and lives his or her life in a positive, caring manner.

Another way to know God is to talk to Him directly. How can

you do this? Some call talking to God prayer. Speak to God as a friend. God doesn't expect big words. Say what's on your mind and then give Him a chance to answer. God sometimes answers in opportunities that arise apparently from nowhere. God's answer may be in the form of something someone else says to you or an idea that comes to you.

Grades

Three things could be happening in your house regarding grades; your parents wish you made better grades, you wish you made better grades, or both you and your parents could be happy or unhappy about your grades.

Grades are meant to be a gauge by which you, your parents, and your teachers can see what you have learned. You can use grades to your advantage. Do you need to spend more or less time on a subject? Are you learning in class? What? Why or why not?

Grades are a common area of arguments between teens and their parents. Many teens feel their parents put too much emphasis on grades. Parents are concerned that teens don't realize the importance of grades. A middle ground needs to be found. First, grades are not the most important thing on earth. One the other hand, they are not useless either. Most disagreements about grades at your house could probably be settled if you and your parents would sit down, discuss your opinions, and reach a compromise. A compromise is better than a continual fight.

Maybe you're the one who is unhappy. Some teens are so hooked on the need for good grades that when they make a bad grade they consider suicide. No grade is worth that! Some suicides occur after a straight *A* student makes a *B* or *C*. Keep the importance of grades in perspective. Other things are more important, like God, family, and friends. Seek help from a trusted teacher or the school counselor if necessary. Ask your friends how they deal with time pressures to get work done or the habit of procrastination.

If both you and your parents are happy with your grades, great! Keep up the good work. But remember, keep a balance in life. Take time to relax and have fun too.

Graduation

Have you ever thought what your life will be like when you graduate from high school? Maybe you have an older brother or sister who has graduated from high school. That graduation may have led you to think about what you want to do with your life.

Graduation from high school is a time most teens look forward to for a long time. The reason? They see graduation as a milestone, an example of something they have done on their own, and an event which will mean they will soon be on their own.

Graduation is a beginning. Yes, a beginning, not just an end. All the plans you have made, the dreams you have had, seem to come to a climax when you graduate. For society it is a way to recognize that you are grown up and have learned certain academic and social skills needed to hold your own as an adult.

The time is never too early to think about what you might want to do when you graduate. You can take steps now to make your future dreams come true. In fact, for some dreams to come true, you need to start thinking now. How are you doing in school? Are you taking advantage of the opportunities that come your way? Don't worry about the future or what you will do. But realize that decisions you are making now will affect your future. Gone are the years when your parents or guardians can control what happens to you.

Do you think you know what you want to do after graduation? It's OK if you don't, but, at the same time, let yourself imagine good things happening. There are things you can do now to help yourself later. (See Exploring, Expectations.)

H

Heroes

Sometimes parents worry about who their teens have for heroes. This doesn't always have to be the case, however. It's good to have a hero. Why? you ask. Take the hero you have for example. What do you like about your hero? Do you wish your life were similar? Why do you like this person or what he has done? While parents sometimes think you want to have every characteristic your hero has, that is seldom the case. More than likely your hero has only one or two qualities you admire and want to have. Even if you don't say out loud that your life could be that way, your hero allows you to dream and wish. Dreaming and wishing are part of being human. A person with no dreams is a person that has nothing to live for.

If you and your parents have a difference of opinion about a certain musician in a rock group or a certain actor or other public figure, ask them about their past heroes. Whom did they admire when they were young? Did their parents dislike that person? This may help them see that your heroes aren't all bad.

Heroes help you dream. Teens use heroes to imagine their lives being different. Teens use them to wish they had the personal characteristics or talent that their heroes have. This is not always bad. As long as you aren't ignoring the rest of your life, it's OK to have a hero. You should. If you spend a great amount of time following what one person does, you've gone too far. Your life is just as important as his, although you may not see that now. Let some of your dreams show you as the main character. What would you do if? (See Dreams, Talents.)

Home

What is a home? What makes a house lived in a home? A home should be where a person can go at the end of the day and find warmth, love, and support. Ideally, what makes a house a home is the caring you find there. Not everyone lives in that kind of home. For some home is more of a battlefield than "life on the outside."

What kind of home do you live in? Is it as you would like it to be? Do you have a good home, or do you live in a home that is nonsupportive of your hopes and beliefs? If you live in a home of love, count yourself blessed. Many teens live in homes where love is not to be found. They are waiting for the day when they can be on their own.

If you live in a home which resembles a battlefield, remember that you don't have to grow as those in your family with whom you can't get along. You can make better choices for your life. When you establish your own home make it one where love is a daily practice. Don't repeat the mistakes of your parents. Do the best you can for now. Find friends and adults outside your home who care for you and live their lives as one should. Get involved with people at school, church, and in community groups who are caring, positive people. One's real home can be said to be where people care about you. It isn't a geographical location or a physical structure. (See Choices, Personal Problems.)

Homework

Homework is a common ground for disagreement between teens and their parents. "Do your homework first!" may be a common battle cry from your mom or dad. Why do parents feel it's so important? One reason can best be shown by using a comparison. Many people like to watch sports and often wonder how professional athletes made it. Besides natural talents, at least one other element was required: the learning of the skills required to play the game. How was this done? Practice.

Homework is like that. It is not something the teachers give to take up your time. Homework gives you a chance to practice what you are taught in the classroom. It is a chance to learn new facts or practice new skills. It is also a chance to practice your mental skills, as you compare, contrast, decide causes, determine solutions. If homework is a problem for you, determine why. Are you scheduling your time well? Use a calendar if necessary. Are you trying to do too much at once? Decide what is really important to you. Drop activities not necessary and/or do them at a later time when you aren't so rushed. Are you having trouble in one particular subject? Get a friend to help, or find a tutor. Homework doesn't have to be a hassle!

I

Impatience

Getting impatient is easy when you are a teen. It seems like years since you were a kid. You're ready to own your own car, make your own decisions, be on your own. Yet it seems some, if not all, of the adults around you still want to treat you like a kid. If only you were old enough to do what you wanted. Use your impatience!

What is it you want to do? Think of something you can do right now that will help you achieve your goal. For instance, you might want to be a professional athlete. Study all the books you can on the sport(s) that interests you. Watch the game in person and on television. Notice the strategy and skills required. Practice the skills needed. Taking care of yourself is just as important. Eat foods that are good for you; exercise to get and stay in shape. Keep your grades up too. Every pro has to retire sooner or later. Injuries end careers early. You'll need something to fall back on, so get that diploma.

Let's say you want to be a business person. Join your local Junior Achievement club or a similar club. Do volunteer work in a business that interests you. Interview someone who has a job that interests you. Take business courses in high school. There are things you can do right now to prepare yourself for your future! Don't let impatience get the best of you. Use it to your advantage!

Infatuation

"But Mom! I love him!" the girl insisted. "You don't know what love is yet," her mom replied. "She's the greatest," he said. "Son, you haven't known her for two months yet," the father offered.

Do either of these conversations sound familiar to you? Teens may fall "madly in love" with each other, only to later find they weren't in love at all. Puppy love is usually a first love. It's innocent and a lot of fun. Infatuation is much more serious for the two involved. They really feel what they have is real love. They may make some decisions that could hurt for a long time.

How can you tell if you have true love or infatuation? It isn't easy because the people who get infatuated are also the type of people who *want* to believe they're in love. It's hard to convince someone of something they don't want to be convinced of. The following questions can help. How long have you known the person, years or weeks? Are you spending every moment possible with your "love"? Instead of concentrating on your schoolwork and other responsibilities, do you find yourself thinking about how great life would be if you were married to this person. How are you handling your other responsibilities?

Infatuation has occurred when two people are unrealistic about what the other person can actually do for them. When you look at two people who really love each another, you see two people who know love isn't a mystery, but hard work! Think you have found your "true love"? Ask yourself the questions listed, and seek the advice of a trusted, wise person. You don't want to make a mistake concerning love. (See Disappointment, Self-esteem.)

Interests

Everyone should have something that interests them. Life is not meant to be work, work, work, all the time anymore than it should be play, play, play, all the time. Other words for *interests* could be *hobby, pastime, recreation, avocation, sideline,* or *ministry.* There are many reasons a person should have special interests.

Your interests can show you what career you might be good in. For example, let's say you enjoy watching sports. Maybe you don't have the physical qualities to be an athlete; but you could become a coach, a sport's announcer, a trainer, a sport's reporter, or a sport's doctor. Many jobs could allow you to work with sports without being an athlete yourself.

You can use your interests as a way to relax from work. As a teen, your work for now is school. Every student should take time to relax from schoolwork. This is a way for you to renew your energies for school. Life should be a balance between work, play, social contact, and spiritual life.

You can use your interests as a way to help your community be better. Many people use some of their spare time to help their community. Youth groups often take on special projects along this line. For example, some youth groups have a community clean-up drive each year. Other groups have dinners for the elderly. Still others put on special safety programs for children. You can do many things to help other people and make your community better as a result.

Until you graduate, school should be your primary concern. Any special interest activities can help renew your mind and spirit for your regular work and help you find your place in the world. (See Talents, Relaxation.)

J

Jealousy

Jealousy means "wanting something someone else has." Instead of concentrating on what you have and what you can do to gain more on your own, you concentrate your feelings on another person and what they have. Jealousy is often aimed at people who seem to have more of something that you'd like to have—more love, more money, more friends, better clothes, more popularity, and so forth. Jealousy is a feeling everyone has had. What is important is how you handle it. If you find yourself so jealous that your daily decisions are affected, you need to look at what is happening.

If you are often jealous, ask yourself why. "Why am I spending so much time concerned with what others have?" Instead of concentrating on other people's lives, do something with your own. Any time you start wanting what someone else has do two things. Decide if what they have is all that great and worth the price you'd have to pay for it. If it is, decide what you can do to earn what they already have.

You can use jealousy to make yourself move and gain dreams that would become lost if you didn't take action. Don't let jealousy rob you of your place in the world! Don't let it keep you from accomplishing the dreams you can have. Test your jealousy to see why it's there, then take whatever action is necessary to get your life back on track!

Jobs

Many teens get jobs before they graduate. These jobs may be part- or full-time during the summer, or part-time during the school year. Baby-sitting and mowing lawns are traditional jobs for young teens to start with until they are old enough to work at fast-food places or grocery stores.

Teens work for several reasons. Some teens work to contribute to the family budget or to save for college. Other teens work to have spending money. Having a job can give you confidence. It can help you discover what job skills and talents you have. It can help you understand how the business world works and where your place may be. Working can help you realize the importance of staying in school to learn the academic skills necessary for the job world.

If you decide you need to work, you need to take some precautions. Seek advice from your parents, a family friend, or a trusted teacher. Look at what working has done in the lives of your friends and other teens in your neighborhood. If you are considering getting a job and aren't sure if you should, think carefully about why you feel you should work. Be sure you are doing it for the right reasons.

Working has its disadvantages. You may find you can't schedule your time well. Working may interfere with your schoolwork. You may start to ignore your friends and family. A paycheck can't substitute for family, friends, or getting a decent education.

Having a part-time job is one way to explore the world and

yourself. If you decide to work, keep work in its place. Only then can you truly benefit from working. (See Volunteering.)

Justice

"There's no justice in it!" This comment is heard when someone is angry that her idea of justice didn't occur. Perhaps she expected a jury to return a guilty verdict or a capital punishment sentence, and it didn't happen. Has something ever happened that caused you to think justice wasn't done? This will probably happen at some time in your life. The idea of justice has to do with what people consider to be right. What a person considers to be right involves her beliefs. A person's beliefs have to do with why she does the things she does.

You can look at justice in two ways. You may know a student who cheats on tests. She is, for now, getting away with it. Even though you want something to happen to her now, it may be years before she gets the consequences or results for her action. Short-term justice would be for her to be caught and given a *F* now. Long-term justice will happen if she isn't caught. The time will come when she can't cheat. She will have to take a test and pass it on her own. Because she hasn't been studying and doesn't know the subject as she should, she won't do well on the test. She isn't really getting away with anything; she only thinks she is.

When we say justice has been done, what we usually mean is what we thought should happen did happen. Justice is bigger than that. What is right is just. Right is a big idea. To know what is right sometimes means looking at the big picture of things, not just what we would like to happen now. What does justice mean to you?

K

Kindness (to Others)

Some people are kind to themselves but are terrible in their behavior to others. There are a number of reasons people are unkind to others. Such persons may be mentally ill, prejudiced, lacking in self-esteem, or unaware of how they are affecting others.

People who are seriously mentally ill can treat others in brutal and sickening ways. These people need professional help to change their behavior. Some people have chosen a value system which allows them to pick on certain other people in ways they wouldn't want to be treated themselves, and they try to excuse their behavior by false assumptions. Some people feel so bad about themselves that they treat others unkindly. Instead they should concentrate on feeling better about themselves. Lastly, people can be unkind to others without realizing it. For example, if they are unaware of how others are feeling, they may say something that is taken the wrong way.

Do you find yourself often being unkind to others? Have you ever tried to figure out why? It's not always easy to look at what you need to change, but if you can it will make you a better person. It is easier to treat others with kindness when you feel good about yourself. People are available to help you learn why you act as you do and how to change.

Are you not sure how to act? Treating others as you would have them treat you is an excellent guide. This is a rule of behavior found in many religions. In Christianity it is called the Golden Rule. (See Kindness (to Self), Self-esteem.)

Kindness (to Self)

For some the hardest thing to do is to be kind to themselves. They can be more understanding toward others. While they will give another person a break, they won't do the same for themselves. People like this often have low self-esteem. In simple terms, this means they have a hard time feeling good about themselves. They sell short their worth as persons.

One of the reasons people are not kind to themselves is an unrealistic set of standards. You expect more of yourself than you do of others. Setting high standards is not wrong. However, keep in mind that you are human. Being human, whether you like it are not, means you will make mistakes. You can expect too much of yourself by trying to do too much at one time or expecting perfection at whatever you do. Set goals. Everyone should have goals. But set realistic timetables to achieve them. Instead of getting upset if events don't work out exactly as you predicted, determine why and learn from the experience.

Learning how to balance work and play is one of the tasks of growing up. Your body and mind aren't supposed to go full blast all the time. Look at your body like a car's engine. A good driver knows that he must take care of his or her car. Keep it clean, check the parts for wear and tear, change oil and filters when needed, and make use of a mechanic when needed. You are different from a car in that your mind can affect your body, and vice versa. You need to put good, clean material into your mind, just as you need to watch what you put into your body. You can't be replaced with next year's model.

You are one of a kind. Treat yourself as such! (See Quiet Times.)

L

Laughter

Life without laughter is like life without love, a meal with no taste, a rainbow with no colors. Laughter should be a part of one's life. Laughter is sometimes called "the best medicine" because of the good it can do for sick people. It's good for people to have fun.

Laughter should be the result of good humor. Humor at the expense of someone else is not good for the person being laughed at or the person making the joke.

Of course, you will have times when you don't feel like laughing. For the most part though, you should be able to have a good laugh occasionally. You can also laugh about things now you couldn't before. Remember how you acted the first day you were in the seventh grade? You can laugh about it now; but then, no way! You were nervous and excited all at the same time.

Can you think of anything more fun than being with some of your best friends, sitting around having fun, and laughing? Being able to laugh is like relaxing and quiet times. It helps rejuvenate you. It's a way to be able to go back to the duller things in life. It's good for you. (See Relaxation.)

Losing

People, teens included, sometimes see losing as the result of a contest one has entered. If you don't win, you lose; if you don't place second or third, you lose. This is only one way of looking at losing.

Only for the narrow-minded is losing seen as a result of competing at some event and not winning. Winning or losing at life is far more important than winning or losing a competition. Life is far more important than a contest or sporting event.

What makes a person a loser? In the long run, losing is an attitude, not a result. You are a loser if you quit. A winner keeps going, sometimes against great odds. A loser refuses to learn; a winner sees learning as a part of the game. A loser sees a competition as everything; a winner see the whole picture.

The person who wins is the person who can endure without becoming bitter. The person who wins is the one who can deal with the problems and conflicts life deals. The person who wins is the one who sees the whole picture. The winner will have sad times, but they don't keep a winner down. The winner keeps with a winning attitude. (See Overcoming.)

Luck

"Boy, does that person ever have good luck!" Think again. Are you sure? Some people would argue that there is no such thing as luck. A person makes her own luck. What am I talking about? Don't I know that some people are lucky? They have all the breaks. Their parents are rich. They live in the "right" neighborhood. Look how good-looking she is. And smart! I'd have to study all night long to make the grades he does without studying at all.

Have you ever felt that you don't have any luck or have little luck? It's not uncommon to feel that way. But you want to avoid the attitude that others "have it made." Living day to day with that kind of thinking hurts you two ways. You're putting your mental energy into feeling sorry for yourself when it would be better placed taking action to help yourself. A particular person may have a chance to take advantage of a situation you don't automatically have. For example, his parents may have "connections." Those connections aren't worth anything, however, unless the person sees the opportunity *and* takes advantage of it.

You can make your own luck two ways. Realize "bad" luck happens to everyone. The person who learns to make even bad luck work for him has the advantage. Second, make your own good luck. Take steps now to reach your goals. Make it happen! Be ready when opportunity knocks. Learn to see opportunity in everything!

M

Mistakes

Made a mistake? Congratulations, you're human! Welcome to the real world. People make mistakes. It comes with the territory of being human. Say you make this mistake often? Perhaps something is going on inside (subconsciously) you haven't recognized yet. Maybe you need to sit down for a moment and see what seems to lead to these mistakes. Does a particular person always seem to be present? Is a certain place always the location? A particular time of the day? If you can't see a pattern, find a trusted person who can help guide you in a positive way. One of the mistakes too many people make is refusing to get help when it is needed. Getting help is a smart move, not a dumb one. But you should try to choose your helper wisely.

How many mistakes are too many? In general, don't keep count of the mistakes you make. If you are trying to learn, to live from day to day by a reasonable set of priorities, you will make mistakes. The only time you should really worry about the number of mistakes is if you are making the same mistake all the time about the same thing. For example, if you are constantly failing to get your homework done, take a look at what is going on. On the other hand, if you occasionally make mistakes and just haven't learned to live with them, you don't have as much to worry about. Living, breathing human beings, going about their business day to day, will make mistakes. What you can do is try to prevent stupid mistakes. Mistakes that could have been prevented if you looked at what was going on.

The only mistake you can make about mistakes is to expect to not make any and to refuse to learn from the ones you make. (See Perfection.)

Money

Money is often a controversial subject. The reason is people's opinion of its place in life. The fact is, money is something a person must learn to handle or it will handle the person. Money can be used wisely or unwisely, just as many other items can be used wisely or unwisely. How you view money and how you use it determines whether you have a control over it or it over you.

Teens often worry about money because their parents do. Others may decide they never want to worry about money, so they become obsessed with making it. Others see so much greed that they determine that the only "correct" attitude about money is to not want it. None of these attitudes is truly wise. Money is a necessity, but one can develop a balanced attitude toward it.

Not every person is expected to take a vow of poverty. A Christian, for example, is expected to pay his way in the world and can do this without becoming obsessed with money. At the same time it is OK for a Christian to make a lot of money if he is making use of the talents God gave him in a way he can be proud of. He can also use part of his money to help make the world better. Christians with money can do much. They can help in ways people with less money can't.

What is your attitude about money? Are you discovering and training the talents you have so you can get a job which not only adds something positive to the world but also allows you to take care of the responsibilities you will have as an adult? Wise choices about one's career and how to handle money can prevent many problems.

Moving

Moving can be a very difficult time for a teenager. Friends are very important, and making friends is not always easy. In our society, people move often. Adults may change jobs four times during their careers, with some people changing more often. Knowing families move doesn't help much when you are losing your best friend and have to start at a new school.

You can help yourself start over. Moving doesn't have to be the end of your life. Look for other new students; they're in the same boat you are. Look for and join clubs that you belonged to in your old neighborhood. Buy the local paper and look at the ads to see what's happening. Get your parents to drive around the neighborhood to see what is available in your new hometown.

Give Mom and Dad a break too. They are starting over just like you are. Just because they are adults doesn't necessarily mean they make friends easier than you do.

Cherish your old friends, but make new ones too. Life has much to offer. (See Exploring, Changes.)

Mystery

Life is a mystery in many ways. What is it about a baby that turns even a tough man into a tender, loving father? What is a rainbow, really? How does it help to dream at night?

Someday you will understand many things about life that you don't understand now. There are also things no one understands, mysterious occurrences that baffle even the wisest person. Being in awe of life is good. Curiosity is one trait adults often lose that they wish they hadn't. It keeps life from being boring.

What strikes you as mysterious and baffling? Why are you so curious about it? Life can be like a good mystery book. You don't know what is happening, though you can guess, until the end of the book. Usually what you thought was the answer, wasn't at all. Sometimes you were close, but the author of the book gave the ending an unexpected twist.

How can your life be like a mystery? Have you ever thought of it that way? Many adults end up doing things they never thought they could do when they were children or teens. If you could do anything in the whole universe, what could you imagine it to be? (See Dreams, Future.)

N

Never

Never is like *always*. It's a word that should be used carefully. There's a saying, "Never say never." Why? Because when you do say *never*, you often end up doing what you said you'd never do. There are some things you should never do, like use cocaine or drive in the dark with no headlights. But there are times when you want to say *never* when you could say *yes*. *Never* is sometimes used in anger. "I'll never be her (his) friend again!" Sometimes it is used when you feel that there is absolutely no chance for you to have something or be something you'd like very much. "I'll never go to college. I don't have the money." Or, "I'll never be as smart as she (he) is." *Never* is also used when you don't think something is possible, even if it is.

If there is something you'd like to have, but don't think it's possible, try this. Just for the moment think very hard about how a person gets what he wants. Instead of using generalizations (things people normally believe), think about what a person really has to do to get what he wants. Break it down into steps. Now, without saying, "It's impossible," think of ways you could take those steps. Remember, even a big project is made up of small steps. Decide what you can do to make your hope come true. Do what you can now. Never just might not exist after all. (See Plans, Opportunities.)

No

No is a good word to practice using. As you have grown older you have had to make more decisions on your own. Peer pressure has sometimes reared its ugly head. You want to belong, but when you do something wrong to belong it bothers you. One of the most important words you can start to use is *no*. You don't have to give a reason; just say no. Say no to such things as dangerous dares, misguided revenge, drinking and driving.

As an adult you will find you have to stand up for what you believe. Practice now. The more you practice saying no the easier it becomes. And when you say it with conviction, you might be surprised at how fast others believe you. Sometimes you have to use the word with yourself as well. "No, I won't eat another piece of cake." "No, I won't watch another hour of television. I'll go visit my friend." "No, I won't buy this album I don't really need. I'll save my money for college." No doesn't have to be said with anger or meanness. Just use it plain and up front. Then turn around and walk off if you need to. The people you were talking to will get the message. And they'll sometimes wish they had your courage. (See Yes.)

Nutrition

Why include the word *nutrition?* Many teens are known to be junk food addicts. In your hurry-up world of "let's do everything today (and don't slow down)," much of the food you eat is what nutritionists call junk food. Junk food is defined as food that fills you up for a short period of time, yet satisfies few, if any, of your body's needs.

Lets think about a race car driver and how his pit crew treats the race car. Whether you are a fan of race car driving or not, you know that the pit crew helps keep the car in the best shape possible so the driver has the best chance of winning. This is a good comparison, or analogy, because many people your age are trying to "win the race of life" and are going at top speed. Imagine what chances the driver would have if his crew put old oil in his car instead of new or put old tires on the car or gasoline that wasn't right for his specially made car? This is what you do to your body when you put food in it that doesn't have the kinds of vitamins and materials your body needs. Your body is still growing, and it needs the best "fuel" you can provide. The wrong food for too long can "clog it up" and even cause damage.

This doesn't mean you can't eat junk food occasionally. It only means that you should be giving your body the nutrition it needs. A pit crew can make a new car after a wreck. Your body is an original, one-of-a-kind, can't-be-replaced model.

O

Opportunities

Your whole life is an opportunity. Every person is capable of doing something positive for herself and her community. Get rid of the notion that you must be rich, pretty or handsome, a brain, talented in music or math, and so forth. Part of growing up is discovering the qualities and talents that make you special. Opportunities exist for each person to make use of her special gifts. The catch, if there is one, is to be able to notice opportunities when they occur.

Opportunities can be defined as occasions when you have a chance to do something you would like to do or something you should do. You may be able to develop computer programs and want to learn more. If you don't read the newspaper, you may never read about the new computer club forming and, therefore, miss an opportunity to learn more about your gift. Maybe you didn't make the basketball team this year. Instead of moaning about that missed opportunity, you can take advantage of a new opportunity. Join a local recreational league or practice on your own and try again next year. Meanwhile keep your grades up.

There can also be times when you can do something you need to do, although you may not be anxious to do so. Opportunities exists that stretch you as a person. For instance, your youth group is planning a trip to a senior citizens' home. You don't want to go. Your grandfather lives in such a home and it depresses you to see him. Go! Don't miss this opportunity to make someone else feel good.

Make your own opportunties by taking advantage of the chances that come your way. Stay aware of what's happening around you. One closed door doesn't mean all doors are closed; look for the ones that are open. (See Yes.)

Organizations

An organization is usually a group of people who have joined together to accomplish a particular goal. Some organizations are profit making (to make money); others are nonprofit (those not wishing to make money).

Your school is an organization. So is your church. Some other organizations you may know about are 4-H clubs, Girl Scouts, parks and recreation departments, and clubs like Future Farmers of America. Organizations may be local; they exist only in communities like yours. They may be national with local chapters. Your dad or mom may belong to Toastmasters, which has local, state, national, and international meetings.

Usually teens use organizations for one of two reasons. One, you may have to. You go to school at first because the law requires it and then because you know it is good for you. You go to the hospital because you are sick. You can also belong to an organization because it lets you do something you feel is important. Maybe you belong to your church's youth group. You can learn while, at the same time, making friends and even doing special projects for your neighborhood. You might have a hobby which has a group or organization you can join.

Another type of organization exists to help youth. Teens have problems, big problems sometimes. Not all teens can talk with their parents. Organizations exist to help you. Look in your local Yellow Pages, and you will find many places and organizations available to help those in need.

Need help? Someone is waiting to help. Want to volunteer? Organizations exist which could use your help.

Overcoming

You can overcome or be overcome. Overcoming means learning to adjust and live with a change that is unwanted and unexpected. Being overcome means something so terrible happens that, instead of doing the best you can and going on, you let this terrible event change your life for the worse.

Terrible times happen to everyone, some time or another. We'd like to be older when some things happen, like having a parent die. But we don't have a choice. When something terrible happens, at least two reactions are possible. You can let it get the best of you, or you can become determined to win out in the end. Sometimes it may be awhile before you feel you have won, but, in the end, you are the winner.

Let's say your parents have divorced. At first you don't believe it. Then you think, *Maybe they'll get back together.* Finally you realize it's final. They aren't going to get back together. You have to make a choice. Do the best you can. Try to adjust to all the changes that have and will take place. Sometimes just take one day at a time and try not to worry. Then your life will start to feel like it has some regularity to it. You have won when you make your life the best you can and you realize their divorce was not your fault.

Terrible things are not just for older folk. Terrible things happen to teens too, like the death of a friend or the death of a parent or an accident that paralyzes someone. You are capable of doing more than you think. You can overcome anything that happens to you. (See Courage, Organizations, Questions, Why?)

Overload

In your rush to do all you'd like to do, you can overload yourself. Overload occurs when a person is trying to do too much at one time. He or she has set unrealistic expectations, often without realizing it.

One result of overload is that you do everything poorly. Another result of overload, and a more dangerous result, is burnout. Burnout is something that happens to people who care about what they do, try to do too much at one time, and wear themselves out physically and mentally. People used to think only adults could burn out. Now people are realizing that teens can burn out too.

Burnout can be prevented. Keep up with the commitments you make. Buy a calendar and mark the days you have tests or papers due or meetings or other commitments. Leave time for relaxing and having fun. Schedule those times in if you have to! Keep a balance between school, family, friends, church, and other outside activities. If you find you've taken on too much, drop something. Ask friends or family for advice if needed. In trying out new things, you may find some things are easier than you thought, others are harder and take more time. Part of growing up is discovering what you can do.

Not everyone has to worry about overloading themselves. Some teens don't try enough new things. Just keep in mind that your teens years are a time to explore and be aware you have limits. Learn to live with stress and get help if you need it. If you have trouble and overload yourself, you aren't the first and you won't be the last, either. Just as burnout can be prevented, it can also be cured. (Quiet time, Relaxation)

P

Parents

Problems between parents and teens are so common that parents almost assume that when their child becomes a teen problems will happen. This doesn't have to be the case. Sure you will have little problems. Everyone has those. You're growing up and getting used to making more decisions. Your parents are having to adjust to the fact that you are growing up. You aren't a little child anymore. One reason the teens years are often difficult is because parents and their teens are going through a lot of changes together. It's the big problems that cause so much trouble.

Problems between teens and parents are of two varieties. You do, or don't do, something your parents wish you wouldn't do or would do. For example, "If your grades don't improve this quarter, you can't try out for the basketball team!" How about, "Take typing instead of chorus. It'll do you good." The second kind of problems occur when your parent does, or doesn't, do something you don't, or do, want them to do. For example, one or both parents may be alcoholic and you want them to go to Alcoholics Anonymous or some other group to get help. Another example of problems parents have that affect their children is a parent who is out of work and has given up hope of finding a job or a parent with a mental illness who needs help.

Problems come in two kinds, no matter how old you are. You can have a problem you can handle by yourself or with friends and family, or you may need to seek the help of a professional, someone especially trained to help. If you or your parents have a problem like this, get help. Start by looking for someone you trust in your family or at church or school. Help is available. (See Organizations.)

Peer Pressure

One of the hardest things you may ever have to learn to handle is peer pressure. You know what it is. It's already happened to you. It happens when a friend, or someone pretending to be a friend, pressures you to do something you don't want to do. They may make it worse by calling you "chicken" or "coward." They might even pretend they won't like you anymore if you don't go along.

Peer pressure can be "harmless." "Get the red sweater, not the blue." Harmless is put in quotes because it's not ever good to make a decision because someone is forcing you to. The worse kind of peer pressure happens when what someone wants you to do is something you know is dangerous. "Just a sip [of beer]. It won't hurt you." "Just try a drag [of marijuana]. Everybody does it."

The best way to prevent peer pressure is to let people know you make your own decisions. If they don't want to be your friend, it's their loss, not yours. You know people like that. You couldn't imagine anyone ever forcing them to do something they didn't want to. Another way to fight peer pressure is to feel good enough about yourself to be able to make your own decisions. When a person doesn't feel good about himself, he sometimes will do almost anything to be accepted. It's your life. If you go along and something bad happens, it's your life that's damaged, not theirs. True friends let you make your own decisions. When you stand up for what you believe, without being ugly about it, you just might be surprised how many others wish they could do the same thing. (See Courage, Friends.)

Perfection

Are you trying to be perfect, maybe without realizing it? There is a delicate balance between trying to do the best you can and trying to be perfect. It isn't always easy to see.

For example, you may be trying to make straight As at school. There is nothing wrong with this if you realize there is more to life than grades. Some people get so caught up with grades that if they make a B they feel they have failed. Failure occurs in having not tried. Bs are fine.

Trying to be perfect generally leads you to be a worrier. You can't enjoy life anymore. You worry about what will happen if . . . .

Try to do the best you can, without making it everything. Life is meant to be fun too. It can't be if you are worrying about it.

No one can be perfect. It's the kind of goal to strive for. Something to aim for, not something to arrive at. Do the best you can, but have fun too. Be kind to yourself. (See Mistakes, Relaxation, Worry.)

Personal Problems

One fact many teens have trouble believing is that other teens have the same problems they do. Every person has some problem with which they must deal. Life, even when things go well, can hand you a situation that must be faced whether you like it or not. Even if you don't have something terrible happen to you, like the death of a parent or a horrible accident or a chronic illness, other kinds of problems occur.

Here is an idea that may help you understand how to deal with problems. Problems can be divided into two types: situational and developmental. You may already have an idea what situational problems are. These problems are the result of a particular situation. Some examples are: your parents divorce, you move from one town to another, or your school drops the tennis team —the one team you wanted to be on. Developmental problems are called that because they are the result of actions, tasks, or times every person must grow through. Some examples are: the first day at school, deciding upon a career, making friends, learning how to speak in public, or getting used to how your body is changing.

Not every event in a person's life has to cause a problem. Part of growing up is learning to adapt and adjust to the way life changes. If a change causes a problem, you may be able to handle it alone. Decide why it is a problem and what must be done to solve it. If you can't solve it yourself and no one you know can help, health professionals are ready and willing. Many hotlines have been established to help people in need. Your telephone book will list these hotlines and other numbers you can call.

Remember two things: Other people have had the same problem you have, and you can learn from them how to help yourself. (See Organizations, Overcoming.)

Plans

Maybe you think it's too early for you to be making plans for anything, but it isn't true. Without realizing it, you may have already made some successful plans in your life. Remember the summer camp you wanted to go to, but your parents said you couldn't unless you saved up half the cost? Remember the steps you took to make the money? Those steps made up a plan. How about the time you wanted to make the soccer team? You knew it took stamina to make the team since soccer doesn't have the time-outs football and basketball do. In order to increase your chances of making the team, you wanted to improve your stamina. Part of your plan was to start running every day. You even talked your best friend into running with you so it would be more fun. Again, you took steps to make your plan work.

Each plan is made up of steps, actions you must take to make your plan work. When it seems something you want is impossible to get, break down the goal into steps. This makes it easier for you to see what you must do. It also is a way to help you achieve your goal. This idea of breaking a goal down into parts is a method used by adults to accomplish tasks at work and at home. It can work just as well for a person your age.

Plans help you schedule or put your life in the kind of order necessary to do things you'd like or need to do. Plans help make dreams come true. (See Dreams, Exploring.)

Q

Questions

Every person has questions he'd like answered, from the small child just starting to explore his world to the senior citizen who has experienced life to the fullest. A common question, but not the only one, is, "Why?"

As with problems, questions can be big or small. They can be questions for which you know how to find the answer. Or they can be questions you badly want answered but don't know where to start.

Some questions have several answers that will work; for instance, "How can I get more exercise?" Other questions, like "Should I drop out of school?" have only one answer. Some questions have only one answer though at first we think there are several. Others have several answers when we only think one exists. The hard part is knowing which is which.

Whether you find the answers depends on a number of things. Have you searched for the answer, or are you just taking the first thing you find out as the truth? Are you questioning what you are discovering, or are you taking it at face value (what seems to be true)? Who or where are you looking for the answer? Some people will lie to you to get you to do what they want. Some people tell you something they think is true that isn't. Some really don't know.

Seek answers from those whose life reflects, shows, that they know what they're talking about. Seek answers from places that reflect the same values you have. Check out the answers to make sure they make sense. If you are in a hurry, you may overlook something you would see if more time was taken.

Any answer you decide upon should not go against your values. If the answer seems impossible, don't throw it out immediately. Give it a chance. (See Answers.)

Quiet Times

Quiet times are important. It is good for you to have a time and place for yourself—a time when you contemplate and rest. Quiet times give you a chance to reflect, to think about what is going on in your life. You can determine what needs to be done next. You can reflect and enjoy the success you have had. Some people have a hard time knowing what to do when they are alone. They are not comfortable with themselves. This is not good.

If you haven't already, find a time and place you can use as a quiet time. Use this place as a getaway, as a place that allows you to get to know yourself better. Learning to listen to yourself allows you to feel, to sense if something is going wrong. It is a time you can really think about what you believe and what you want. It gives you a chance to make wise decisions, not hurried by peer pressure or pressure you place on yourself in public.

A solitary place can be in your home or elsewhere. It is more an attitude than a place. It is an attitude or place that allows you to relax and enjoy yourself for awhile.

Everyone needs quiet time. It helps make the actions you take work out better. (See Relaxation.)

R

Rainbow

A rainbow says many beautiful things about the world that are true.

A rainbow is something that causes people to pull off the road and look at it, forgetting all their worries for a moment. People of all ages can enjoy the beauty of a rainbow. You should always take time to relax and enjoy life.

Rainbows are multicolored. Could you ever imagine a rainbow with no colors or only one color? Have you even complained because you wanted something about yourself to be different. Imagine if blue wanted to be red or yellow wanted to be green. The things that make you different make you special. The world needs all the specialness that exists.

Rainbows stand for hope at the end of a storm. Everyone goes through storms of life. There is light at the end of the tunnel. In other words, there is hope. Rainbows can remind us that better times are on the way.

A rainbow is one of those special things that make life worthwhile. (See Mystery.)

Relaxation

If you are physically healthy, you have one less problem to deal with in your life. Who wants more problems than they already have? People can be physically unhealthy in different ways. For example, you can be born with a physical problem, or you can live in such a way that you cause yourself physical problems.

One way people cause themselves problems is by rushing through life, full-steam ahead, not taking time to rest and relax. Taking time to rest and relax is not the same as taking time to sleep. In addition to sleeping, a person also needs to give his or her body and mind a chance to renew itself. Sleep alone isn't enough.

Do you take time to relax? What do you do to relax? One way to relax is to exercise. Those who have stressful jobs often find exercise relaxing, though that doesn't sound possible. Isn't exercise tiring? There are two kinds of tiredness, physical tiredness and mental tiredness. A person with a stressful job uses up his mental strength. To relax, and get away from work, this person exercises. He is using physical strength then, not mental strength. Notice that people with jobs based on mental tasks usually pick pastimes that involve using physical abilities. People whose jobs are more physical may pick pastimes which involve more mental exertion.

What do you do to relax? How have you found it helpful? (See Quiet Times.)

Religion

Since the beginning of time, people have felt the need to believe that a greater power knows what is going on and is in control of things. As a result many religions exist in the world. People have always searched, but not everyone has come up with same answer.

The word *religion* has different meanings to different people; just as the various religions practiced have resulted in its followers living a variety of life-styles. You can look around at your schoolmates and find many different life-styles and values.

What does the word *religion* mean to you? What religious beliefs do you have? Does your life show those beliefs?

Different religious beliefs have been used to separate the world. Do your beliefs do that? Or do your beliefs give hope and attempt to reunite the world? How?

What does it mean to you for a person to have "religion"? What kind of difference should it make to them? Or you? (See Questions, Unbelief.)

S

Self-esteem

Self-esteem means feeling good about yourself, who you are and what you can do. Everyone needs to feel good about himself. Only those who can are able to get along with others.

You are living through a period of time when you will probably be harder on yourself than ever before or again. Teens usually have very high expectations about themselves and others. It is very important to look good, have friends, belong, fit in. Take, for example, the extremes teens go through to wear the "right clothes." This kind of peer pressure has existed in every generation. Yours is not the first.

Teens want to fit in for a reason. They want to be accepted. Being accepted means you have worth just by being you. You can have self-esteem without always going along with the crowd. For teens this is hard because you are just discovering who you are. It's hard to know what to stand up for when you don't always know how you feel. You are going through a time when you are no longer a child, yet not an adult. Sometimes you feel grown-up, but other times you feel like you're still a kid. Much about your life is a mass of confusion. But one thing stays basically the same, your peer group. The friends you hang out with are always there. Your friends are going through the same basic growing pains you are. You just don't always realize it.

Feeling good about yourself occurs more easily if your parents love and encourage you. It helps if you have good friends too. Even if this isn't the case you can still feel good about yourself. Try to learn something each day. Be good to your family and friends. Make the world better each day by being you. (See Mistakes, Talents, You.)

Shyness

You're shy and think it's a dreaded social disease. Maybe you feel OK about it but your parents are trying to get you to be outgoing like your brother or sister. Maybe you'd like to be more outgoing. But it isn't easy.

You may be more than quiet; you may actually be shy. Or you may call yourself shy when you just haven't had a lot of practice getting along with others. There is nothing really wrong with being quiet and less talkative than others. Being quieter has some advantages. You see and hear more than someone who is talking all the time. You might, however, feel you should be able to make friends or be able to speak in class more easily. You can do this by getting more practice. Find chances to practice. Practice with a friend. Take small steps at first. As you have small successes, add new challenges.

If your parents are pressuring you, decide if your parents worry you might miss out on something. Do you think they are concerned because they want you to be someone else? It might just appear that way. They may be geniunely concerned about you and may think you'd be better off being less shy. Try to help them to understand how you feel. Show them you still have friends. Show them you are taking steps to be more confident.

You might feel you could have more friends or be more accepted. Take a look around you, a good look, and you will probably find someone else who is shy who has friends. Having friends depends on how you treat people, not how loud you are. Being shy is not a disease. Many people are shy who appear to be confident. Some movie stars are shy but don't appear to be. You can become more confident. Take small steps and give yourself a chance. (See Friends, Jealousy.)

Sisters

Do you have a sister? Sisters disagree with each other, as much as brothers disagree with sisters. Some, of course, disagree or fight more. There are a number of reasons for this. No two families are exactly the same, even if they have the same number of sisters and brothers.

Sisters and brothers are a topic parents may groan about when brought up for discussion. "I wish they would get along better," is not an uncommon comment from parents about their children. Why do sisters and brothers fight? Part of the reason may be competition for their parent's affection. Children sometimes feel that the amount of time parents spend with them equals how much they are loved. Part of the reason for this thinking may be the fact that a person is not born knowing how to get along with others. Since sisters and brothers grow up together, they see each other when they are still learning how to live—how to get along, how to make friends, how to communicate, or how to agree or disagree.

Fact is, it shouldn't seem wierd if you fight with your sister occasionally. If it happens a lot, you need to look at why you fight and do something about it. No one likes to go home to another fight week after week. On the other hand don't think too badly of yourself or your sister if you do fight some. Just remember, there will be a time when you will grow up and leave home. Your sister will too. Wouldn't it be nice if you could depend on each other then? Friendships with sisters, or brothers, are just like other friendships; they must be worked at. How are things going in your house? (See Brothers.)

Suicide

Suicide is something some teens contemplate. Teenagers try to kill themselves, and some succeed. If life gets you so down it doesn't seem worth living anymore, stop. There are people who care about you and want to you to live! If you die, it is a great loss! Life is full of ups and downs. Depression, sadness, boredom are all feelings people have at one time or another in life. Feelings, all kinds, are part of life. After every storm comes a rainbow.

If you ever feel life is hopeless, find someone with whom to talk. In addition to close friends, you can talk to a family member or school teacher whom you respect and trust. You can also talk to your minister or school counselor. Your community may have a mental health center. Many communities have telephone hotlines you can call anonymously (you don't have to give your name). Some communities even have special teen hotlines. Find someone who will listen to you! Stay alive!

T

Talents

Everyone has special talents or gifts. Your talents, together with your personality, make you different from anyone else in the world.

What? You haven't discovered anything you'd called a talent? Some people's talents are more readily noticed than other. Part of growing up is discovering what talents you have.

Many kinds of talents exist. People commonly think of artistic, athletic, and musical talents when they think of gifts. These are actually only a few of the talents that exist. A person can be talented in academic fields like math, science, or foreign languages. People can also be talented in social skills, such as the ability to lead, the ability to understand different people, or the ability to speak in front of groups.

Two facts should be realized no matter what your talents. Talent must be trained and practiced, and talents are meant to be used. You can do this by staying in school and taking courses that will sharpen your gifts. Also read on your own, watch others with the same gifts, and have a hobby that develops your talents. College or some other kind of post-secondary education will be needed to put some talents or gifts to use.

Putting your talents to use is smart for a variety of reasons. Your talents are natural for you. In using them, you will gain self-confidence. Everyone has a place in the scheme of things. Using your talents fills a space only you can fill. When you use your talents, the end result is a happier you. Talents also prepare you to learn even more. That is why those who have special gifts often appear to have many talents. Be proud of your talents. They are what make you special! (See You.)

Teachers

"But, Mom! My teacher is the worst!" How many times have you had a teacher you just "hated"? You may have even begged your mom or dad to ask the principal to transfer you to another class. You may have a teacher who shouldn't be teaching. In that case you should calmly speak with your parents and give them a point-by-point explanation of why you feel as you do. Then it is up to your parents to investigate and get something done.

Anytime you feel you don't like a teacher, ask why. Is it because you don't like the class? Is it because the teacher doesn't seem to like you? Is it because of the way the teacher teaches? When you determine why you don't like the teacher, you can take action to adjust to or change your situation.

Teachers are not in your school to be friends, although it is more fun if they are friendly. Teachers are there to teach the class you're taking. Don't let the personality of your teacher keep you from learning what's important in that class.

Teachers can teach one very important lesson which doesn't have anything to do with the subject they're teaching. They can teach you how to get along with a variety of people. When you grow and enter the work force, you will most likely find you can't control the people with whom you work or for whom you work. Learning how to tolerate and get along with your teachers will help you learn to get along with the variety of people you will met in your life. Don't expect to like all the teachers you have, but take the opportunity to learn what you can from them. (See Opportunities.)

Tests

You've already taken a lot of tests in your life. You take tests at school to show what you've learned in class. You may have taken tests to determine if you have a learning disability or to determine if you learn better one way or another. You have even taken what are called intelligence tests. Tests are usually used as a gauge, a way to determine how much you have learned or how much you might be able to learn.

Tests, in general, make people nervous. Being prepared is the best way to handle a test at school. If it is a big test, get enough sleep the night before and don't wait until the last moment to study. Some students use a calendar to mark when tests are going to be given and use it to determine when they need to study.

Tests make some people so nervous they actually get sick with headaches or stomachaches. Tests aren't meant to make you that way. A person who gets too nervous about tests usually places too much emphasis on the importance of the test results. If you get this way about tests, ask yourself why. What is it that makes this test so important that you have a physical reaction? If you can't find a way to handle tests by yourself, ask for help. Talk to a teacher or counselor you respect or any adult who can help you understand why you feel the way you do. Tests are only tools, a way to help you. They aren't meant as a torture chamber! (See Grades.)

U

Unbelief

There are basically two kinds of unbelief. One occurs when a person does not believe and never has. This kind of person may be afraid to search and discover the truth. She may have been taught to believe as she does. She might never have had the chance to discover what she doesn't know. Judgments shouldn't be made about someone who doesn't believe. Your example should be the kind that lets the unbeliever ask what you have that she doesn't have.

The other kind of unbelief occurs when you have believed but something happens to make you wonder if what you believed was really true. Asking questions is natural for people. It's part of what makes you human. You need to be honest when you have a question. Events can happen to you which cause you to think about what you believe. When this happens the best thing to do is to ask questions and search for the answers. Don't feel guilty about how you feel. Use your doubts as a chance to explore and learn things you didn't know before!

A third possible occurrence is a person who doesn't know what to believe, but is searching for the truth. Everyone is in this position at one time or another. One of the hardest things you must do is to decide for yourself what to believe. The time comes when you can't use your parents as an excuse to get out of doing something others want you to do. You must decide for yourself. Learn to ask questions, search for the answers, and test the answers you find. (See Answers, Questions, Why?)

Understanding

There are two ways a person can understand. A person can understand a subject like algebra or a word like *salient*. A person can also develop the ability and desire to understand people and their emotional, social, physical, or spiritual needs. To understand others means that you can see why they feel the way they do or act the way they do. To be understanding doesn't mean you agree with how they feel or what they do.

To be understanding you may have to use more wisdom than the person with whom you are dealing. Only people who can show mental, social, and spiritual strength can be understanding. This is why a person with understanding can act independently of how others may feel. He or she has the ability to separate the doer from the deed.

The benefit of being understanding is at least threefold. (1) Problems are prevented. You can take steps necessary to solve the problem or prevent one from happening if you understand what is happening. (2) You can show others a better way to act and live. People won't change until, or unless, they see a good reason for it. When they see what happens in your life because of your ability to understand, they can decide it's a good way to be. (3) People who are able to see "the whole picture" are the kind of people you'd like to have as friends. If you have understanding, you can more easily gain other people's respect.

Are you understanding? Being understanding isn't always easy. Note: Sometimes the hardest person to be understanding of is yourself. (See Kindness [to Self], Feelings.)

V

Vocation

What you do for a living can be called your vocation. It might also be called your career. It is best to work at a job you enjoy. This makes you and those around you happier. It also means you will be better at what you do. Almost every person has to work at some time in his life. To decide on what job you should have, determine what you like to do, what you are good at, what you are trained for or can be trained to do, and what opportunities exist where you live.

You can explore in many ways your skills, talents, and likes to determine where you can work as an adult. How you do at school is important, though you don't have to make straight *A*s. Join clubs and play sports if you like. Get experience by volunteering. Get out in the world and explore all the possibilities. Visit the science museum, watch educational television channels, read good magazines and books, pick a hobby, enjoy the hobbies of friends and family, observe what is happening around you. Particularly notice people who are enjoying their lives and what they do for a living. You may or may not have the same talent as they, but you can still learn important lessons from them. The world has a great variety of people, things, and ideas in it. Browsing the magazine rack at a library or book store will show you just a few of the activities people like and make a living or hobby out of.

You can assume that you will have to learn your entire life, if for no other reason than to be able to stay in the job market.

Every person in this world has an important place to fill. That includes you! The key is to allow yourself to discover that place! (See Books, Exploring, Volunteer.)

Volunteer

Being a volunteer is one of the best things a person can do. People in need are helped, and those helping make their community stronger.

One of the ways volunteering can help you is that you can gain confidence. It is a chance for you to discover what you can really do. Success (being able to do) grows into more success (the willingness to try new or more tasks). Volunteering is a chance to try out something without a long-term commitment.

Many places can use volunteers. Your youth group at church may have its own special volunteer project. Clubs and organizations at your school might have such programs already established, or you might suggest they do so. Organizations within your community have a regular need for volunteers. Training also exists to prepare you for what you will do. If you are interested in volunteering, ask your parents, youth leader, teachers, counselor, or friends if they know what is available.

Volunteering can help you discover the type of career you might like to have. It gives you a chance to explore and train your special gifts. You can practice social skills. You can gain a better understanding of how the business world operates, indeed, how the world is. In addition, you can feel good about yourself. You will be helping people in need. Not too many activities offer so many benefits to so many people. (See Opportunities.)

W

Why?

Why did it have to happen? Why did it happen to me? Why did Joe kill himself? Why did all those people have to die? Why didn't we win?

In times of trouble, "Why?" is a common question. It may seem essential that you get an answer. If only you had the answer, somehow you feel you could go on! You may forsake everything else for an answer.

Events happen because of commission and omission. Commission means someone did something he shouldn't have done. For example, a person who dies of a overdose took drugs and killed himself. Or a person who takes a dangerous dare may end up getting hurt. Omission means a person didn't do something he should have. A person may need to take certain medicine every day. If he forgets, he may have a seizure, faint, or worse.

If something bad happens, the reason may be obvious. David had a wreck and died because he was driving too fast. You didn't get the scholarship because you weren't involved in enough activities. You can make sure you don't make the same mistake David made, and you can join a new club and apply for another scholarship.

Sometimes things happen that seem to have no rhyme or reason. These are the hardest events with which to deal. In these cases, you must learn to live without an answer to "Why?" Take advantage of the situation. Look at your life and how you are living it. Is there a lesson for you? Is there something you need to change? Do you have your priorities straight? Learning to live without answers to "Why?" is a sign you are growing up. You may want an answer badly, but you live on without it. This is one of the hardest lessons of life there is! (See Answers, Overcoming.)

Winning

Winning is a topic discussed often in today's world. You can think about winning in two ways. Winning can refer to how a person does in a contest, or it can be used to define a person's attitude toward life.

How do you become a winner? First you must learn how to try. You must be willing to take a chance, but you chose your chances carefully. You learn to act according to your own values, not others. You learn to get along with others without giving up your own values. Winners are people who add something to the world. They are not the kind of persons who take and never put something back. They remember their friends and families.

Persons win with the right attitude. Winners don't quit. Winners are willing to take on great challenges, to do things no one has done before. Winners are not concerned with other people's opinions; they are more concerned with what is right.

A person can be a "winner" and a "loser" at the same time. How? Let's say a young man wins a junior tennis tournament. However, in so doing he acts rude to the other boys he beat and perhaps is even rude to the spectators. In the long run, this winner is actually a loser. Who wants to be around someone who can't or won't be considerate of others?

How do you win? You win by being persistent, enduring, and looking forward. Competition, in and of itself, isn't bad. How you act as the winner is what is important. What did you learn from the competition, and how did you treat others? A real winner is glad others win too. (See Losing.)

Worry

Is worry a problem for you? Do you worry about when you'll be asked out for the first time or when you will first ask a girl out? Do you worry whether you'll get mean old Mr. Wilson for P.E. or the fantastic Mr. Jenson? Do you worry about everything or nothing in general. Do you constantly worry?

Worrying about something in particular isn't too much to be concerned about. You might worry about grades, friends, your parents, college, just about anything that can concern a teenager. Instead of needlessly worrying, do something! What can you change? How can you do it? A little worry is a normal occurrence in a person's life. What is the difference between being able to change things and having to learn to live with it? If you can't decide that on your own, find someone who can help you. You can change worry into action.

If you worry too much, or seem to be worried all the time for no particular reason, you should be concerned. This is not healthy. Worrying too much or too often can have a negative effect on your physical health. If you find yourself worrying too much, figure out why you are worrying. Get a friend or someone else you trust to help if necessary. Worrying isn't meant to be a everyday experience.

You can conquer worry by asking why and taking action! Banish worry from your everyday life. (See Change.)

X

eXcitment

What gets you excited? How do you feel when you're excited? Being excited about life in general is great, and almost every person has something that gets him excited.

When you are excited, you may have other feelings too. For instance, you may be excited about your team's game today, but you may also be scared. Feelings sometimes come in pairs. When you win you may become scared that you might lose the next time. When a person accomplishes a goal he has long worked for, he may also feel down. To get rid of this down feeling, the person will need to set another goal. Excitement may be paired with a feeling that seems weird and out of place. Fear and excitement may occur at the same time. Conflicts in feelings can worry a person who doesn't understand that he can have two feelings at the same time. You aren't crazy; you're human. Listen to your feelings and what they tell you.

If you believe you haven't anything to be excited about, take another look at your life. Maybe something bad has happened and you need to give yourself time to heal. Perhaps something is wrong and you need to talk with a wise adult and find a way to bring excitement to your life. You don't have to be excited all the time or get excited about everything, but you should have something in your life about which you get excited. (See Zeal.)

eXtremes

Going to the extremes is something teens seem to be known for. Some teens do things just to drive their parents nuts, so to speak. "If John (Jill) doesn't stop soon, I'm going to have to say something. It has gone too far." Teens go to extremes because they are often willing to be the first to do something new. At first it may seem extreme, but after a while people get use to it and it becomes normal. For example, teens may be the first to try a new fashion. Soon, however, the new fashion becomes an old fashion and a new, new fashion starts. Many times teens go to extremes because of peer pressure. You do something to be accepted, to belong, even though you know it is extreme. You can also do something to the extreme without realizing. This is why it is important to think about the possible results of anything you do.

Some kinds of extremes are dangerous. Too much of anything isn't wise; too much food, too much speed, too much sleep, too much exercise, and too much worry are some examples. Some extremes are just silly; like wearing the same jeans five days in a row, always wearing pink, or never eating the crust on pie.

In fact, teens don't go to extremes anymore than other age groups do. When an adult goes to an extreme he or she isn't always noticed. No parents live with them. No brother or sister tells on them. Their children may not know what is happening is extreme.

Regardless of age, doing something to the extreme can be unwise. Are you doing something to the extreme? Is it potentially harmful to you or someone else? Why do you do it? If you know it is unwise and want something better for yourself, you can change. (See Peer Pressure.)

Y

Yes

Just like *no, yes* can be difficult to say. "Yes, I will volunteer to help at the hospital one night a week." "Yes, I will mow the lawn this spring." "Yes, I will try out for the school play." "Yes, I will be a friend to the new student in class." Saying yes can mean you are doing something you want to do, like going to the movies. Saying yes can also mean you're willing to take a chance on a friendship, on discovering or practicing your special talents, or on doing something new and different. Knowing when to say yes, and when to say no is a big step in one's life. Knowing what's best isn't always easy. Allow yourself to make mistakes, and try to learn from them. The next time someone asks you to do something you know is OK to do, but you aren't sure you can do it, look at the situation. Do you have the time? Will it take you away from another responsibility? Or are you tempted to say no because you're scared you'll look funny or because it's different? Perhaps no is the answer you should give. Perhaps yes will open a new door of opportunity. Which is it?

You

You are important. Every person on the face of the earth has the ability to do something important. If your answer is, "Nonsense, I can't do anything. I'll never do anything great," ask yourself what you mean by that. Not every person can go to the moon or perform open-heart surgery or became a great athlete. Not every person is supposed to. A person can be great in his own community. Real heroes of the world do great things that never end up in the newspaper. Take for instance, the senior citizen who teaches adults how to read, helping them to be able to help themselves and their families better. Or the man who coaches in his spare time and helps kids gain in confidence and ability. Or the teenager who volunteers time at a senior citizen home, playing the piano and singing for the people who live there. Every community has heroes, individuals just like you who use some special ability to make life better for other people.

Some people have an inferiority complex. This means they have a hard time feeling good about themselves. Often they have trouble accepting compliments. They may even make excuses about something about which they should not be ashamed. Maybe you feel this way sometimes. Accepting a compliment doesn't make you stuck-up. No one person is better than another. This world needs everyone to take part. You are just as important as anyone else. You aren't required to be perfect; no one is. Just try to do your best. You are important. Believe it! (See Talents.)

Z

Zeal

Zeal is a word you may not have seen before. It means to be full of enthusiasm, spirit, intensity, and eagerness. Life is meant to be lived with zeal. Notice those people who seem to love life and what they do. Do they go from day to day appearing bored, living in a rut, not interested in what happens? No! They are eager for each new day. They make the most of the time given them. They share their love of life with others. They are fun to be with.

Perhaps your hero has this characteristic. It might be one of the reasons you admire and wish to be like him. You can have zeal too. It is a great attitude to have about living. Zeal is an attitude. Having zeal doesn't mean you don't have down days. But it does mean you have your priorities in order and you know what is really important.

One way to have zeal is to recognize and be thankful for the good things you already have. Count yourself blessed if you have good health, a working brain, friends and family who care for you, decent values, and a desire to make the world better. The next best thing to do to have zeal is to have a dream, something that gets you going in the morning. A reason for living will stir the heart faster than almost anything else. What are you looking forward to? (See Dreams.)

Zits

Zits may be representative of one of the things most important to teens—acceptance. For some reason having a zit stands for ugliness or social unacceptance. What happens when you get acne? Do you panic? Have you tried every advertised remedy on the market to hide the zit or prevent it from happening? Few things so small can cause such a extreme reaction as a teen with a zit before a major event, like the prom.

Acceptance is very important to you. Friends are perhaps more important than at any other time in your life. When, and if, you do get acne, remember two things: You will notice it more than your friends unless you make such a big thing of it your friends can't help but notice, and the zit isn't you. Do what you can to take care of your face, but don't give it more importance than it deserves. Your true friends aren't going to leave you for something as common as a zit. They get them, too, and are probably as worried about getting them as you. Some people do have major problems with acne. If you do, see a doctor. Medicine is available to help.

The best way to be accepted is the way you act and treat people, not an occasional problem with acne. Keep zits in perspective! Your zit isn't the real you! (See Friends, Self-esteem.)

Summary

What would you like to do? Have you made a plan yet? Use the following steps as a way to accomplish something you want. Write how you plan to make it happen. Writing helps make your plan more real and possible. Here are some pages for you to write your plans for change.

Your Plan of Action

1. What do you want to do? List each wish.
   Work on one change at a time.
   _____

2. Make a plan.
   What needs to be done? List the steps necessary to make it happen.
   _____
   _____

3. Act on your plan.
   "Today I will. . . ." "Then I must. . . ." "By (date) I will. . . ."
   _____

4. Evaluate how things are going.

"Step one is done. I need to start step 2 and talk to Mom about step 4."

"The one thing that isn't working is. . . . Maybe Mr. Peters has an idea I can use."

5. Keep on going.

After you see how your plan is working, continue as is or change as needed. Plans often have to be changed. Don't get discouraged.

If you want something to happen, you must work for it! Decide what you want, and do something about it today!

Your Plan of Action

1. What do you want to do? List each wish.
   Work on one change at a time.
   _____

2. Make a plan.
   What needs to be done? List the steps necessary to make it happen.
   _____
   _____

3. Act on your plan.
   "Today I will. . . ." "Then I must. . . ." "By (date) I will. . . ."
   _____
   _____

4. Evaluate how things are going.
   "Step 1 is done. I need to start step 2 and talk to Mom about step 4."
   "The one thing that isn't working is. . . . Maybe Mr. Peters has an idea I can use."
   _____
   _____

5. Keep on going.
   After you see how your plan is working, continue as is or change as needed. Plans often have to be changed. Don't get discouraged.
   _____
   _____

Summary

Important Phone Numbers

Use this page to list telephone numbers you may need, for yourself or a friend.

1. Friends and family

Name   Number

_____
_____
_____
_____

2. Your minister, teachers, school counselor, coaches, etc.

Name   Number

_____
_____
_____

3. Community Resources

Name   Number

Mental Health Center   _____
Teenage Runaway Hotline   _____
Suicide Prevention Center   _____
Ambulance Service   _____
Hospital   _____
Others

Name   Number

_____
_____
_____

Additional Entries

You will find the next few pages blank. Why? So you can add answers to questions and concerns you have which are not included in this book.

These pages are yours.